BE A BETTER
PRIMARY SUPPLY TEACHER

Liz Rhodes

Teach Books Division, MA Education Ltd, St Jude's Church, Dulwich Road, London SE24 0PB

British Library Cataloguing-in-Publication Data
A catalogue record is available for this book

© MA Education Limited 2007
ISBN-10: 185 642 353 0   ISBN-13: 978 1 85642 353 3

Printed in the UK by Athenaeum Press Ltd, Dukesway, Team Valley, Gateshead, NE11 0PZ

BE A BETTER
PRIMARY SUPPLY TEACHER

by Liz Rhodes

TEACH BOOKS

A division of MA Education Ltd

CONTENTS

INTRODUCTION – Why be a supply teacher?

There are many reasons for being a supply teacher. Sometimes it's a default situation at one end of a teaching career. Either you haven't found the job you wanted at the end of your teacher training or you have taken early retirement from full-time teaching, but don't want to give up altogether. It could be a conscious decision to supply-teach for a while, giving you a chance to sample different types of school. You may need the flexible timing that supply teaching offers you to fit in with family requirements.

If you have just finished training, supply teaching can provide you with invaluable experience, but it is a bit like jumping in at the deep end. Until now, you have had mentors, tutors and class teachers to turn to for advice. Suddenly you're on your own. You're deputising for someone who knows their class, is an experienced teacher and has a wealth of resources behind them. Here you are with their class and an A4 page of instructions to last you the whole day.

Even if you have given up teaching full-time, supply teaching can still give you that sinking feeling when the children first come in from the playground. Each class offers you a new situation and you don't have the luxury of being able to take your time in deciding how to approach it. You're thinking on your feet and making snap decisions based on less information than you would like.

So, what are the advantages and disadvantages of being a supply teacher? Many of the answers are the two different sides of a coin. You don't have the overall long-term responsibility for a class, but on the other hand you don't have the professional satisfaction of seeing your class progress. You have a flexible timetable, but you may not get as much work as you would like. You don't have paid holidays and if you're working for a LEA directly, you won't

get paid until the end of the following month. You don't have to spend a large part of your life preparing long-, medium- and short-term planning, but on the other hand you sometimes have to teach a lesson in a very different way from how you would have planned it.

You don't belong anywhere. People are always pleased to see you, mainly because otherwise they might have to take your class. But they are also prepared to dump things on you without any conscience at all. It's amazing how many playground duties seem to come your way. If your class has to go to hymn practice, instead of having that time for marking you are asked to perform some other duty. You are responsible for finding out when things happen. If you don't finish bang on time, you will have angry parents beating on the door.

But at the end of the day, as soon as you have finished your marking, your time is your own. No meetings, twilight sessions, parents' evenings, after school clubs, displays to put up, reports to write, assessments to make, lessons to plan or IEPs to prepare. Your time is your own. And perhaps the best thing is that you have been free to teach, unencumbered by the thoughts of all the other things you will be expected to do. It's a very refreshing kind of freedom.

Box 1.1 Advantages

- conscious decision or default situation
- provides invaluable experience
- no long-term responsibility
- flexible timetable
- no planning, preparation and assessment
- get your weekends back
- freedom just to teach.

In this book the use of he, him or his is gender neutral and is intended to include both sexes.

CHAPTER 1

GETTING WORK AND WHAT YOU NEED TO KNOW ABOUT EMPLOYMENT

There are two ways to find supply work. Either you register with an agency or you go round schools with your c.v. In either case, you will need to have a Criminal Records Bureau (CRB) check and it has to be up to date. You cannot apply for this check yourself. It has to be applied for by whoever is going to employ you - either your Local Education Authority (LEA) or supply teaching agency - and it can take a long time to process, so you need to get it sorted out in plenty of time.

If you have been working in schools as a student or as a full-time teacher, you will already have had CRB clearance, but it does need to be renewed regularly. Requirements are frequently being changed, so for up-to-the-minute information, visit the CRB's website, www.disclosure.gov.uk. When you have CRB clearance, it is not transferable; it does not belong to you, but to your employer (agency or LEA). So if you were to apply for a post with a different employer requiring clearance, the new employer would have to seek fresh CRB clearance.

YOUR CHOICES

There are several agencies you can work for and some are detailed at the back of this book. Some of them concentrate on particular geographical areas, while others operate nationwide. The advantage of working for an agency is that they pay you the week after you have worked, whereas if you work directly for schools, the LEA pays you a calendar month later, ie. you will not be paid for work done on 1 April until the end of May. When starting out and after school holidays, it is a good idea to mix agency work with direct work, so that you can gradually build up to a good paycheque without being stony-broke in between times.

Agencies charge schools more and pay teachers less, but the main reason schools use agencies is (particularly if a member of staff calls in sick at 7.30 in the morning) because they only need to make one 'phone call'.

Depending on where you are on the pay scale, you can expect to get a minimum of £100 a day gross working directly or £85 working for an agency. Obviously, from a budgetary point of view, schools would prefer to employ you directly as they have to pay agencies much more money, but circumstances sometimes dictate that they use agencies.

Agencies do their best to look after both their schools and their teachers. Most of them run websites which will link you to schools' Ofsted (Office for Standards in Education) reports, give instructions and road maps and also keep your personal diary, which you are encouraged to fill in online.

Agencies that work centrally are not always very good at their geography, so if you live in a large county, do make sure you know where they are sending you before you commit yourself. It is a good idea to give yourself a mileage limit if you are driving to work. Or a traffic light limit if you live in a rural area. In any case, nobody will pay you for your time spent travelling or your costs. Decide what works best for you. If you are dependent on public transport, you will need to consider how accessible a school is for you. Most LEAs run their own supply agencies and will be able to put you in touch with them.

Of course you can approach schools directly, in which case you will be paid by the LEA. The best way to introduce yourself is to go into schools where you would like to work. Leave an A4 printed sheet containing details of your teaching experience, a photo to jog memories and your contact details. State what your preferences and particular skills are (e.g. KS1 or 2, expert musician) but do emphasise your flexibility. Schools like a direct approach because it saves them money and it is good to have someone coming in who isn't an unknown quantity. Also, if the school is local to you they can ring you up in a panic at 9.15 (yes, really!) because of some unforeseen crisis. If you contact a school in this way, you are virtually guaranteed work at least once, and after that, it's up to you.

Obviously, once you are in a school you make yourself known to all the people who may be in a position to contact you. The school secretary will probably be the one who books you in advance when members of staff go on courses. The people who ring you late at night or early in the morning are likely to be the head or deputy head, so you need to get yourself onto their mobiles. Usually the school secretary holds a list, which you will

need to sign so that you can be paid. If you are working through an agency, then details will be faxed through to them on the same day.

PAY AND CONDITIONS

If you are employed directly by your LEA or school you should be paid according to statutory rules set out in the *School Teachers' Pay and Conditions Document (STPCD) 2006*, which can be found online at www.teachernet.co.uk (DfES, 2006a). If you work for a whole day, you must be paid a daily rate based on 1/195th of the annual salary you would receive if employed full-time. You can find an up-to-date list of annual and daily pay rates on the National Union of Teachers' website (NUT) www.teachers.org.uk. These change fairly frequently. Check that if you teach for a full day you are paid the daily rate, rather than an hourly rate which may lead to lower total pay. If you work for less than a day, then you may be paid an hourly rate determined by the LEA or school. You should check the pay rate used. An hourly rate of 1/950th of the appropriate annual salary is recommended by the NUT, while the DfES suggest a *pro rata* hourly rate depending on the length of the full working day for other teachers.

The *STPCD* (2006) does not specify the length of the supply teacher's working day but the DfES recommends that the normal working day should be considered as 6.48 hours of working time, or the total length of the school day including an allowance for non-contact time. The DfES also recommends that teachers be paid for all the hours they are required to be on the school premises, and further suggests that supply teachers should be offered the opportunity to be involved in other duties as well as teaching and that this should be accounted for in the salary calculation.

Salary progression, sick pay, maternity pay and pensions

All supply teachers employed by the LEA or a school are entitled to incremental progression on the pay spine each year. They must receive an additional spine point for experience in September each year, provided they have worked during at least 26 weeks in the previous 12 months, until they reach the top of the main pay scale. Supply teachers are also eligible to apply to go through the threshold onto the upper pay scale. The head of the school where you work most will normally assess your threshold application form with appropriate input from the heads of the other schools you go to. You will also be eligible to progress on the post-threshold scale.

As a supply teacher you are not covered by *Conditions of Service for School Teachers in England and Wales* (commonly known as *The Burgundy Book*) the national agreement on occupational sick pay or occupational maternity pay (Local Government Employees, 2000a). *The Burgundy Book* or represents the national agreement between the six teacher organisations and the local education authorities. All employers of teachers should adopt the conditions of service set out in it. (You can access *The Burgundy Book* on the ATL's website, www.askatl.org.uk.) There are, however, some circumstances in which supply teachers may be entitled to statutory rights to sick pay or maternity pay.

If you are working for an LEA you will be able to have six per cent of your pay deducted to contribute to your particular LEA's pension scheme. This is voluntary, so you can decide what works best for you.

SECURITY OF EMPLOYMENT

As you will generally be employed on a day-to-day basis, you will not have the same security of employment as permanent members of staff. If your stay at a school becomes extended, you may be offered a temporary contract. If you decide to sign one of these, be very clear about what you are prepared to do and what is covered – *make sure that everything is written down*. For example, you may be expected to attend parents' evenings, write reports, plan, prepare and assess or run after-school clubs. Supply teachers who are looking for permanent employment often see a temporary contract as a step towards a "proper job" and, if this is the case, it is only sensible to find out what may be available. The DfES advises that supply teachers can only be 'encouraged' to take up extra duties, such as playground duty and that, if they agree to do them, then they must be paid accordingly.

SCHOOL WORKFORCE REFORM

If you are providing long-term cover for a particular teacher, then you should benefit from the same provisions of school workforce reform as the teacher you are replacing. This means that you should have the same Planning Preparation and Assessment (PPA) time and classroom support as the class teacher. (PPA allocates every teacher in every school a guaranteed ten per cent planning, preparation and assessment time) If you are just supplying cover for a day or two, it is unlikely that you will get scheduled PPA time. Regrettably, it is often the case that if you are on short-term supply, classroom support is reallocated; very short-sighted on the part of management, as classroom assistants can be invaluable in helping you to run the class as smoothly as possible.

WORKING FOR AN AGENCY

If you are employed through a supply teaching agency you are not automatically covered by the terms of the STPCD (DfES, 2006a). The agency determines the pay rates and conditions of service for supply teachers they employ. Sometimes, holiday pay is added on. Some agencies offer their teachers the opportunity to join a stakeholders' pension scheme, but you would have to make individual enquiries of any agency you intend to join.

Education employment site Eteach manages supply pools for a number of local authorities who are taking steps to establish supply arrangements that do not exploit teachers. Supply teachers employed through Eteach receive the *The Blue Book – Capital Funding for Voluntary Aided (VA) schools in England 2006–2007 Version* (DfES, 2006b) pay and conditions and have access to a pension scheme. This publication is not available in hard copy but can be downloaded on Teachernet. See *www.teachernet.gov.uk/vabluebook*.

UNION MEMBERSHIP

It is *essential* to belong to one of the teaching unions (details at the back of the book) because, in the event of any difficulties you may have, your union will be there to support you. Some scenarios include injury while at work, disputes about your duties as a supply teacher (although this is unlikely; they just won't ask you to go back) or, most seriously, allegations by pupils. In the event of any problems it is vital to have your union's backing, especially since they will cover any legal costs. Union membership is offered to supply teachers at reduced rates, based on how much you hope to work each week.

WHEN YOU GET A BOOKING

When you get that call, you need to be able to think quickly. Firstly, find out where the school is and how long they want you for. (You will have to decide whether you are prepared to work for half days or not.) If you want to or can get there, then ask what year class you will be teaching. Get the school's exact address and telephone number and if you don't know quite where it is, ask for the post code so that you can look it up on www.ukstreetmap. co.uk. Find out who you should report to when you arrive at the school and ask whether there is work set for the class you will be teaching. Make sure you know what time you will be expected to arrive and ask whether there are any specific instructions for parking. These may all seem rather fussy, but once you have said you'll go, the person who is booking you will be so relieved that they will gladly tell you all you need to know. It is worth asking what themes the class you will be teaching is working on, because you may have some especially good resources.

If you are already booked for the day, don't forget to thank the school for ringing and ask them to call you again another time.

Obviously it is a good plan to use your mobile phone and to leave a message on it saying you will contact callers at the first available opportunity. Check for calls regularly. People looking for supply teachers aren't going to wait long for you to call back; they want to get something sorted out. But if you work regularly with schools and they know that you are reliable, they will usually be prepared to wait for at least an hour or two.

Remember that you are a commodity and only as good as your last booking. If a school finds you are unavailable too often, then it will stop calling. The upside of this is that there are some schools you don't want to call you. Some staff seem quite unwelcoming to supply teachers and, while not actually obstructive, don't go out of their way to be helpful. Fortunately, this is the exception rather than the rule. At the beginning of a new school year you may find that a school you have been going to for some time has made different arrangements; they may have taken on someone permanently to cover PPA time and will 'borrow' them for the occasional day's supply. Unfortunately it has been agreed that classes may now be taken by people who do not have Qualified Teacher Status (Cover Supervisors) and this, again, may cut down on the opportunities available to you.

Handy Hints

- You will need an up-to-date Criminal Records Bureau check, which needs to be applied for by your employer.
- Agencies pay you the week after you have worked (roughly £85 a day).
- LEAs pay you at the end of the month after you have worked (about £100 a day).
- limit yourself as to how far you will travel to a school: you aren't paid for your time or your petrol.
- Approach schools directly.
- Make yourself known to contacts at school – secretary and deputy head.
- Make sure you are paid at a daily rate rather than an hourly one.
- You are not usually eligible for sick pay or maternity leave as a supply teacher.
- You may elect to pay into an LEA pension scheme.
- If you sign a temporary contract, make sure that everything that is covered is written down.

cont./..

- Supply teachers may only be 'encouraged' to do extra duties. If they agree to do them, then they must be paid pro rata.
- If you work for an agency, they determine pay rates and conditions of service.
- You must belong to a teaching union.
- Check your mobile frequently or, even better, have someone at home to take your bookings.
- Remember that schools change their arrangements, so you can't depend on continuing to work at a school, no matter how often you have worked there in the past.
- When you accept a booking find out:
  1. Where the school is (exact address and phone number).
  2. How long the booking is for.
  3. What year you will be teaching.
  4. If work is set.
  5. What time you should arrive.
  6. Whether there are special parking arrangements.
  7. Who you should contact when you arrive.

CHAPTER 2

KEEPING ON TOP

There is a big danger of becoming de-skilled if you have been a supply teacher for a long time. New initiatives, new technology and new strategies all conspire to make your knowledge and abilities out of date. It is therefore your responsibility to make sure that you do keep abreast of educational developments.

EDUCATION INITIATIVES

You need to be aware of new educational initiatives. These are always structured in the same way and each one addresses:

- The purpose of the initiative.
- How it is structured and who is involved.
- School-based activities that will affect your role.
- Information and support to which you should have access.

You will be able to find out about new initiatives on www.dfes. gov.uk. This site contains a wealth of information and has an excellent search facility.

A good way of keeping up-to-date is to get on your union's mailing list. Most of the unions run courses in different parts of the country, so ask them to let you know when anything is being run in your area. These courses are usually free, or you might be charged a small nominal fee.

If you are doing a lot of supply in one school, keep an eye out for notices of future in-set days. These can be very useful if, for instance, the whole staff is being taught how to make the most of interactive whiteboards. Headteachers are usually very pleased to let you join in on these sessions, though of course you won't be paid! But you do get the double bonus of learning something and showing how keen you are.

Probably the most important help available to you is the series *Self-study Materials for Supply Teachers: Pack* (DfES, 2002a). These were originally published in book form, but are now only available for downloading online. Of course this enables all the material to be updated whenever necessary and you can pick and choose what you do want to download.

The self-study materials have been specially written to improve supply teachers' knowledge and skills. The materials consist of five books, which provide supply teachers with a foundation resource to address gaps in their knowledge. The five books are *Getting Started* which includes information on special educational needs, English as an additional language and inclusion; *Core Subjects in Primary Schools; Core Subjects in Secondary Schools; Classroom and Behaviour Management;* and *Filling the Gaps* (2002a), which includes information on personal, social and health education, citizenship and ICT in schools. You can view the books on the Teachers section of the DfES' Supply Teachers' website: http://www.teachernet.gov.uk/supplyteachers/ or download them directly.

Box 2.1 Top Sites

The supply teachers' website http://www.teachernet.gov.uk/supplyteachers/will give you loads of material and good advice. Also, check out www.dfes/standards/gov.uk for government initiatives.

The self-study book *Getting Started* (2002a) discusses four vital areas:

- teacher learning and development
- meeting the needs of all pupils
- professional responsibilities and legal liabilities
- educational initiatives and issues.

There are many other useful downloads available. One that is particularly interesting for those returning to teaching is the *Course For Supply Teachers, Returners to Teaching and Teachers from Overseas* (DfES, 2001a). This publication contains training and notes on the *National Numeracy Strategy (NNS)* (DfES, 1999a). The training is intended for those teachers who have no previous training in the *NNS* and the materials offer an overview of and give teachers a chance to become familiar with the *NNS* approach to planning, together with an explanation of the structure of the daily maths lesson. Effective strategies for teaching maths are also discussed.

TEACHER LEARNING AND DEVELOPMENT

All supply teachers will have gone through initial training and induction and will have Qualified Teacher Status. While these will have provided you with the essential skills to begin your career, it is recognised that Continuing Professional Development (CPD) is vital for maintaining an up-to-date knowledge of curriculum subjects and making the most of new technologies. QTS Standards set out the professional knowledge, understanding, skills and attributes, which are necessary to enter teaching. You can find the QTS Standards at http://www.tda.gov.uk. The DfES document *Teachers' Standards Framework* (2001b) covers the expectations contained in the national standards for:

- knowledge and understanding
- planning and setting expectations
- teaching and managing pupil learning
- assessment and evaluation
- pupil achievement
- managing resources
- managing own performance and development
- managing and developing staff and other adults
- strategic leadership
- relations with parents and the wider community.

You can use the framework to help you decide whether you meet each of the expectations under the ten headings, though obviously the last two will not usually be appropriate for supply teachers.

The www.teachernet.gov.uk site also lists development and funding opportunities for CPD aimed at:

- helping teachers to manage change
- improving the performance of individuals and institutions as a whole;
- increasing staff morale and sense of purpose
- leading to the personal and professional development of teachers
- promoting a sense of job satisfaction
- pulling together a school's vision of itself
- raising standards of achievement in pupils at all levels.

MEETING THE NEEDS OF ALL PUPILS

This is particularly difficult for supply teachers, because meeting individual pupils' needs depends so much on knowing the children. Even if you provide work differentiated at three levels, this only gives blanket coverage. In spite of recent statements, inclusion is certainly with us for the foreseeable future. The DfES document *Transforming Secondary Education (2001c)* explains the challenges of inclusion that you are likely to encounter classes containing children who '...experience barriers to learning as a result of their disability, heritage, gender, special educational need, ethnicity, social group, sexual orientation, race or culture...'

Box 2.2 Inclusion help

It may be helpful to visit www.qca.org.uk/ca/inclusion or www.nc.uk.net for an overview of inclusion. Have a look at the Special Educational Needs (SEN) Code of Practice (DfES, 2002b), which states that children with SEN should be offered full access to a "broad, balanced and relevant education...".

If you are doing long-term supply in one class, it would be useful to look at the *National Curriculum Handbook for primary teachers in England (DfES, QCA, 2000a)*, which outlines how teachers can modify National Curriculum (NC) programmes of study to provide all pupils with relevant and appropriately challenging work at each Key Stage. In reality, you will have no prior knowledge of children in your class with Special Educational Needs (SEN), but it is suggested that you respond to pupils' diverse needs by:

- Creating effective learning environments.
- Securing their motivation and concentration.
- Providing equality of opportunity through teaching approaches.
- Using appropriate assessment approaches.
- Setting targets for learning.

In practice, you will find that very often a child with SEN will have a designated classroom assistant who will have a special programme of work for that child. But don't depend on it; very often this support is part time, and you will find it can be withdrawn at different times.

If you do notice anything about a child (whether special needs or not) that gives you cause for concern, then you must leave a note about it for the class teacher. This could be something the child says, does or writes, or, an unexplained bruise. The teacher won't mind if you point out something she already knows about and will appreciate the fact that you have shown awareness and concern.

Classroom Assistance

You will often have support in the classroom. The term "teaching assistant" (TA) includes learning support assistants (LSAs), classroom assistants and others whose primary role is to help the teacher in the classroom. The presence of this kind of support has been shown to make a significant contribution to improving standards within a class. LSAs are often closely involved with the lesson planning for children with SEN. Classroom assistants will support children who need extra help, for example a less able group in literacy or numeracy lessons.

SEN Help

At the time of writing there are several well-established programmes designed to help less able children. Teaching assistants play a vital role in their implementation and will often have received training in the delivery of these programs. Early Literacy Support (ELS) is for year 1 children, and Additional Literacy Support (ALS) is for years 3 and 4 pupils. Children may also be supported by specialists in English as an Additional Language (EAL) teaching. In addition, the *National Numeracy Strategy* offers the Springboard programme which is intended for those Key Stage 2 children who have a weakness in number work (DfES, 1999a).

Gifted and talented

Gifted children are identified as those with high ability in one or more academic subject, and talented children have high ability in sport, music, visual arts and/or performing arts. As such, they should be given the opportunity to study appropriate subjects in greater depth and at a faster pace. These children need encouragement and support so that they can develop emotionally, physically and socially in line with their talents.

The following strategies are recommended to meet the needs of gifted and talented (G&T) children:

- Use of pupil grouping within the classroom or the school to ensure that G&T pupils have some opportunities to work with others of similar ability.

- Extension, where pupils are following a common curriculum but the most able use more challenging resources and are asked questions that require higher levels of thinking.

- Enrichment, which gives pupils learning experiences beyond the normal curriculum e.g. primary children might be offered an opportunity to learn a foreign language or visit a theatre.

- Acceleration, where gifted or talented pupils move out of their peer group and work with older pupils either for all lessons or in one or two subjects. When accelerating, care must be taken to accommodate the child's emotional and maturation needs.

- Study support programmes before or after school, during lunch hours, at weekends or during the holidays. These might include participation in the national programme of G&T summer schools.

- A separate homework programme for some pupils, providing more opportunities for in-depth study and greater flexibility in the way a topic is tackled.

■ Pastoral support for unhappy or isolated G&T pupils.

There are several programmes in place to support the teaching of G&T children and these can be found at www.standards.dfes.gov.uk

English as an Additional Language

EAL is the term used when referring to children whose home language or mother tongue is not English. Policies of inclusion insist that EAL children should have the same access to the National Curriculum (NC) as their peers. It is important that you show that you value their language and cultural differences, and obviously you have to make allowances for their lack of English when setting tasks. But do have high expectations and expect the children to contribute as much as they can. At first they will absorb the language and may not speak much. The Ethnic Minority Achievement site (www.standards.dfes.gov.uk/ethnicminorities/) will provide you with support and it contains advice on raising achievement, collecting and using data, good practice and answers to frequently asked questions. Depending on the school and how many EAL children there are, you will find that there is a variety of staff to can work alongside the children in class, help with planning and support them appropriately.

PROFESSIONAL RESPONSIBILITIES AND LEGAL LIABILITIES

You will find details of conditions of teachers' employment at www.teachernet.gov.uk/pay. Supply teachers working directly for a school or LEA are subject to these conditions, but if you're employed by an employment agency you work according to your contract with them. Many of the responsibilities itemised will not affect you as a supply teacher, such as report writing and attending parents' evenings.

Assemblies

Attendance at assemblies is usually required for administrative purposes.

Directed time

Directed Time covers the hours that teachers must be available to carry out their duties (under the direction of the headteacher). However, it does not include the amount of time required for preparation and marking, which will depend on how long you need to take for these. All teachers are entitled to a break in the middle of the day and lunchtime supervision is not normally part of a teacher's contract.

Ofsted Inspections

If an inspection takes place at the school where you are working, you may be observed. If you are at that school for five days or more, you will be given individual feedback on your performance.

Physical restraint

Physical restraint of a pupil by a teacher using "reasonable force" is only allowed to prevent a child from:

- committing a criminal offence
- injuring themselves or others
- damaging property
- acting in a way that is counter to maintaining good order and discipline at the school.

Full details about what is permissible can be seen at: http://www.teachernet.gov.uk/teachinginengland/detail.cfm?id=226

Sanctions

Sanctions should be used in accordance with the school's behaviour policy. This will usually be displayed in the classroom, but if you're not sure, ask someone to explain the rules to you.

Child protection

Child protection is a part of your job. You are taking the place of the class teacher and are responsible in that capacity but as a supply teacher your role is to inform the school's designated member of staff if you suspect that a child is suffering from abuse or neglect. You must not attempt to investigate the matter yourself and, should a child confide in you, you must not guarantee confidentiality. Explain that you will only tell people who need to know in order to help. For more information, visit www.nspcc.org.uk where you will get a comprehensive overview on the child protection system in the UK.

Physical contact

Physical contact with pupils is not illegal; in fact, it is inevitable when working with younger pupils. But do bear in mind that innocent contact can be misconstrued, or even deliberately misrepresented. It is therefore sensible to avoid touching children or being alone with them in confined or secluded areas. If you have to talk to a child on a one-to-one basis, either make sure another teacher is present (not taking part in the conversation) or go to a public part of the school where there are plenty of other people around.

Health and safety

All teachers have a duty of care towards their pupils, especially in terms of health and safety. Make sure you know the fire drill and don't block the fire exit in your classroom. You should be continually carrying out risk assessment, which will come as second nature, and generally act *'as any prudent parent would'*. Both schools and LEAs should have specific guidelines for potentially risky activities, such as swimming or some design projects involving the use of sharp tools. Make sure you know what the guidelines are, and if you are in any doubt at all about the safety of an activity, ask for appropriate advice.

Public liability insurance

This insurance is held by all schools, which means that teachers (including supply teachers) are covered against third-party claims arising out of school-based activities. As long as you haven't deliberately acted illegally or dishonestly you will normally be covered by this insurance. If you agree to look after pupils' property (e.g. watches during PE sessions), then the property becomes your personal responsibility and any loss may not be covered by the school's insurance. So make sure that anything of value is kept in a safe place. If you take pupils in your own car or use your car for school business, you must check that your motor insurance policy covers you for this.

Equal opportunities legislation

Equal opportunities legislation applies to supply teachers. The Equal Opportunities Commission (www.eoc.org.uk) has been created to deal with gender discrimination. The Commission for Racial Equality (www.cre.gov.uk) addresses matters of racial discrimination and the Disability Rights Commission (www.drc-gb.org) attends to disability issues.

Anybody, including children or those acting on their behalf, may make a complaint to these bodies if they feel that they have a grievance.

As a professional you have to understand your contractual and legal obligations and your rights and entitlements. This is quite a minefield, so I can only reiterate – *make sure you are a paid-up member of a teaching union!* Of course, most teachers will go through their entire careers without encountering any problems of this nature, but you should be prepared in case of any misunderstandings.

Handy Hints

- Get on the mailing lists of organisations which may run courses.
- Be aware of in-set days in schools and ask to attend them if appropriate.
- Be aware of downloads available and check for new ones.
- Provide differentiated work where possible and appropriate.
- Use 'differentiation by outcome' to cover some projects, particularly those in humanities.
- Be aware of both SEN and G&T children and provide for them as necessary.
- Understand the needs of children who have EAL.
- Directed time does not include the time you need for marking;

- You are entitled to a mid-day break: lunchtime supervision is not normally part of a teacher's contract.
- You may be observed if your school is having an OFSTED inspection.
- You may use "reasonable force" to restrain a child to prevent him from injuring himself or others, damaging property or committing a criminal offence.
- Check out the school's behaviour policy so that you know what sanctions and rewards to apply.
- Child protection is part of your remit, but only in an advisory capacity – always consult the appropriate member of staff.
- Avoid physical contact with children and make sure you are not alone with a child.
- Check the fire drill arrangements and do not carry out any activity if you are unhappy about safety aspects.
- Schools are insured against third-party insurance claims, but if you accept children's valuables for safe-keeping, then they are your responsibility.
- If you use your car for school business, make sure that your motor insurance policy covers you for this.
- Be aware of equal opportunities legislation, which applies to gender, race and disability issues.

CHAPTER 3

A SUPPLY TEACHER'S DAY

Basically, while teachers in schools are friendly, they are busy people and expect you to understand how their school works, within reason. Every school has its own agenda for day-to-day running and you will need to know about how registers are taken, annotated and delivered to the office, how dinners are sorted out, what the arrangements are for playtimes, dinnertimes and wet play and the routines for assemblies. Some schools provide supply teachers with a handout explaining all this, which makes life much easier, but unfortunately that is the exception rather than the rule and you will have to find out how your school's day runs. Always look for the timetable which should be on the classroom wall. It is useful if the class teacher leaves you the password for their laptop so that you can use the inter-active whiteboard, but as yet this is something that teachers usually forget or are unwilling to do.

WHAT THE SCHOOL SHOULD SUPPLY

The NUT suggests that schools should at least:

- Greet the supply teacher and give him a "welcome pack".
- Provide a map of the school to help a teacher find classrooms, staff room, toilets etc.
- Give clear details of main contact person(s).
- Provide a timetable with times of lesson change, breaks and lunch period.
- Contain emergency contact people and telephone numbers or procedures.

- Give details of registration procedures, fire drills and security arrangements, including door codes.
- Outline usual lesson procedures, e.g. arrangements with regard to school uniform, code of conduct, if or when pupils may visit the toilet, class lists, brief notes on pupil ability and seating plans.
- Provide details of photocopier codes, computer passwords and details on technical support.

Unfortunately, it is very rare that you are given all this, but it does give an indication of the things you need to know, and possibly find out, before you start teaching your class.

BEHAVIOUR POLICY

Every school has a behaviour policy and you should look at this so that you will know what the sanction and reward systems are. When you arrive at school people will volunteer all kinds of information, whether solicited or not. All too often it runs on the lines of, 'Watch out for Liam, he's had a dreadful week and hates any kind of change' (that means you!). Make a mental note of the names mentioned, but when you meet the children trust your own judgement because they react differently to different people. Some children have a definite case of teacher-lag: they have become so used to being put down and told off by their own teacher (bear in mind that the class teacher has them for the whole year, which is a long time in the life of a challenging pupil) that they welcome a new and friendly face and will respond well to being given a bit of responsibility and lots of praise.

WHAT'S IN YOUR BAG?

Every good supply teacher will have a stock of resources. Ideally they should be in plastic envelopes in a ring binder and are kept at home so that you can pick out whatever is appropriate. Mine are classified as:

literacy KS1, literacy Y3/4, literacy Y5/6, and the same for numeracy. Then I have a general file for each Key Stage containing science, history, geography, music, art, PSHE and RE. In addition, I have a collection of circle time activities, educational gymnastics, a story board framework sheet and maths puzzles. So, if you are called early in the morning it's easy to grab what you think you might need. This only falls down when you get to school and they've changed their minds and you're teaching Y6, not Reception, but generally it gives you a useful, basic toolkit.

An excellent new website provides lots of information especially for supply teachers. It's called the Supply Bag (www.supplybag. co.uk) and, among other things, has lesson plans for each year group. If you were called out at 8.00am, you could quickly download a few lesson plans to get you through the day. These plans are general and are ideas for you to use on the board; they do not involve photocopying – never the easiest thing to do first thing in the morning in an unfamiliar school. This is a marvelous resource and is very user-friendly.

I also have a (big) pencil case containing:

- whistle
- two sets of 'I have ... who has...?' cards
- laminated set of 'Where? Why? When? What? Who?' cards which can be stuck to the board
- Blu-Tack
- emergency pencils (Ikea ones are good)
- pencil sharpener
- eraser
- assorted ballpoint pens (some schools prefer you to mark in green)
- notes of union membership, teacher reference number, pay reference number and NI number
- various ID cards
- board magnets
- string (cat's cradle for wet playtimes)
- a notebook to jot down passwords for all the photocopiers and school entrances I'm likely to need
- assorted board markers
- money for coffee and lunch
- mobile phone containing important phone numbers.

In my bag I also have:

- a bottle of water
- a CD of *Carnival of the Animals* (good for impromptu PSHE or music sessions)
- a descant recorder;
- a memory stick containing lesson resources and essential for copying good ideas)
- storyboard writing frame
- some circle time activities
- age-appropriate stories and poems.

If I'm teaching Key Stage 1, I try to take a Big Book to read with the children, because it is so much more stimulating for them.

YOUR CLASSROOM

You are shown your classroom and can pick up clues as to how it is run just by the look of it. Are the displays bright and inviting or tired and dog-eared? Are they celebrations of the children's work or posters from the TES? Are they aimed at the children or intended to impress visitors? Is there an overload of information or is it about right for the class' age group? Is the classroom tidy or does it look as if a bomb has hit it? What is the book corner like? (I once came across a book shelf where all the books had their spines facing inwards – not very encouraging for the intending reader!)

Make sure you know where the fire exit is and quickly run through fire drill instructions. (From the number of fire drills that have been sprung on me, far more than the law of averages would lead you to expect, it seems that schools carry out these procedures at least once a week, and sometimes the fire alarm sounds without any warning. Children are generally well-practised at fire drill and will file out of the classroom quietly.)

Usually the class teacher will have left a list of instructions on the desk, but of course in the case of sudden illness this may not be the case. The instructions normally take the form of a timetable with annotations and appropriate photocopies. They are often signed off with "Enjoy!", which the teacher has written before gleefully skipping off.

Now find the whiteboard and a pen that works (always carry your own spares) and write the date (long and short) and your name. It is also helpful to put a brief timetable up, not least because it's easy for you to refer to. Key stage two children usually sit in their places for registration, so it is a good idea to put some mental maths or a word game on the board. Many classes will have silent reading at this time, but don't depend on it. Even if this is the case, there is always the child who 'hasn't got a book'.

> ### Box 3.1 Word Game
>
> Here is a good word game for key stage two children: write a nine-letter word on the board, jumbled up and in three rows of three. Ask the children to find as many words as they can, as well as the nine-letter one, and make sure you have a word which doesn't give the opportunity for four-letter epithets. You can later go over the answers, pointing out that you can use the same word endings with different initial letters, therefore using rhyming capabilities. Most children should be able to get about 30 words as long as you choose something with a good mix of vowels and consonants.

An invaluable source of maths puzzles is *Mathematical Challenges for able pupils in Key Stages One and Two* (DfES 2000c). You can get this free of charge by ringing the DfES on 0845 60 333 60 (code 0083/2000). It contains 83 puzzles at all levels, many of which are easy to put up on the board and are fairly quick to solve. The solutions are at the back of the book.

Registration

When the class comes in (sometimes you are asked to fetch them from the playground) ask the children to sit down quietly in their usual seats or on the carpet. (It is a good plan to have paper and pen available at this time: parents often come in to tell you that their child is being picked up by someone different today, and you need to record this.) Introduce yourself and say that you've been looking forward to coming to this class.

The register comes in many forms. Some classes are registered on the computer and the results are emailed to the office. Some require you to mark only those pupils who are absent. Some are the old-fashioned type, which need to be filled in completely.

Explain to the children that as you don't know them yet, it would be good if they put their hands up as they answer their names. Also, apologise in advance for any mispronunciations you may make – they usually raise a laugh anyway. It works well to say 'good morning' to each individual and expect them to reply appropriately. Sometimes a TA will sort out the dinner numbers for you, but make sure that you record and send to the office any money you may receive. Again, there are many different methods in schools for recording dinners; some children have tickets paid for centrally, while others pay weekly, daily or not at all.

Once all the "housekeeping" is done you can go through the work you have put on the board as a starter activity and when the register monitors have returned from the office you should start your first lesson.

Teaching

Very often your first session will be either literacy or numeracy and will sometimes be set – some of your children will go to parallel classes and other pupils will come into your class. Sometimes you will want them to begin the session on the carpet and work on individual whiteboards. If not, make sure they move to their places quickly and quietly. If any books need to be given out, make sure this is done now and make sure that everyone has everything they need (write a list on the board, e.g. pencil, ruler, homework book, exercise book).

Before you start teaching, it is essential to ensure that everyone is listening and looking at you. No-one should have anything in their hands and they should all be able to see you and the board, if you are using it. Write your learning objective (LO) on the board so that the children have a focus. Explain to the children what they will be doing during the lesson and why. Make sure they understand what you regard as acceptable and unacceptable behaviour in the classroom and ensure that you are consistent about this once you have started your expectations.

Teach your lesson in the normal way, inviting interaction from the children as usual. Don't allow any calling out—strictly hands up. The children know how to behave, but will try it on with a supply teacher, so make sure they understand that you will not tolerate bad behaviour. You need to strike a balance between being firm and pleasant. If a child is persistently disruptive tell him that he is stopping other children from learning and deal with him according to the school's behaviour policy. This may involve sending him to another class with his work or giving him a dinner time detention. Usually there is a system of warnings: you write miscreants' names on the board and it is 'three strikes and you're out'. Children often ask if they can change places, but their teacher has probably put them all in a specific order for a good reason, so it's better if they all stay in their original places.

A system which works well, probably because the children don't expect it, is to write the names of the whole class on the board, in advance. Someone is bound to ask you why their names are there and you can tell them that all the names are of children who are working hard; you hope you won't have to rub any out, but if you do, it is possible to be reinstated with improved behaviour. It's a variant on the old 'catch them being good' theme, so give it a try.

It's important to call as many of the children as possible by name. Some of them, you will learn all too easily and quickly, but you can also read names off book covers or pencil cases and children respond very well to the personal touch. It's easy to learn the names of the naughty, clever or less able pupils, but you will really earn Brownie points for being able to name the amorphous lump of "average" children.

When the main part of your lesson is over you can do a plenary, discussing with the children what they have learned. You will need to mark their work. If the answers are simply right or wrong, you can go through them together and ask the children to self-mark, using a different colour pencil. When they have finished this, or if you are doing the marking from scratch, ask them to leave their books open where they have been working and put them in a tidy pile on the table. This means that you won't have to spend hours finding their work and it will only take a minute to collect up the different piles. It also means that you are cutting down on movement within the classroom. Make sure that each group of children is sitting quietly before you dismiss them.

SCHOOL DAY

Schools arrange their lessons in different ways. Some get two sessions in before break, one after and then assembly before lunch. Others have one long session, an earlier break and then two more lessons afterwards. Afternoons should be broken up into at least two sessions, with time for a story at the end of the day. Quite a few schools now recognise the merit in having an afternoon playtime for the whole school, even though it means finishing a bit later. It gives the children a chance to expend some energy; otherwise they are in the classroom for more than a two-hour stretch. If you don't get an afternoon playtime, it is often possible to take your children out unofficially just for a few minutes. It makes a big difference to their levels of concentration if you can do this.

In case you can't get out, or after a wet playtime, here is a good activity for any key stage two class. Write the alphabet in capital letters in rows and columns across the board. Under each letter write "l", "t" or "r" (for "left", "together" or "right". Explain that you are all going to chant the alphabet and at the same time you will raise the appropriate arm (or arms), given by the instruction under the capital letter. Everyone needs to stand up and face the board to do this. The first time you do it, go quite slowly and then repeat a bit faster. The children find it is much more difficult than they thought it would be and enjoy the challenge. It also helps to prepare them for the next activity.

Playtimes

Usually someone will tell you if it's your playtime duty, and apparently it very often is! There is usually a rota up in the staffroom, so do check on it. If you are on duty, hopefully it will be with another member of staff. In any case, try and position yourself where you can get a good view of the playground and so that no corners are hidden from view. If you're not on duty, take the opportunity of going to the staffroom and grabbing a coffee. Do ask where you have to pay if there is no obvious tin and make sure you don't use anyone's special cup or sit on a designated seat!

After play the children will continue their lessons until dinner time. Quite often there will be an assembly during the morning. You should accompany your children to this and join in unless you are specifically told that you aren't needed. If that's the case, you can use the time to get some marking done or prepare something for the next session.

Dinnertime

Dinnertime is officially your free time, but it doesn't always work out like that. Each class has access to a Meal Time Assistant (MTA) whose duties include supervision of meals and the playground. Sometimes children eat their packed lunches in the classroom. It isn't your job to make sure they leave the tables clean and tidy, but it may be in your interests to do so if no-one else does. This is the time when you can eat your lunch (you will get to know which schools provide good value and wholesome meals) and get up to date on your marking. Also make sure that you are prepared for the afternoon's activities. This may involve raiding the PE cupboard for equipment or making sure you have the necessary tools for an art session. If you need to borrow keys to get what you need, always be sure to give them back. It sounds obvious, but you want to build up a reputation in schools for being reliable and competent, and forgetting to return keys is a cardinal sin.

Afternoon

Many classes start the afternoon with 'silent reading'. If this is the case, make sure each child has an appropriate book (no sharing) and explain that you are going to make use of this time to listen to readers so you need it to be really quiet. Take the register quickly and then go round the class, with a chair, listening to readers. Make a note of the children you listen to unless there is a specific list to work from. A useful rule of thumb is to go to the children reading big print first, as they will need more practice!

Don't let the reading session go on for more than 15 minutes. Ask the children to put their books away (or in their reading folders) and start your afternoon lessons. Sometimes the whole afternoon will be taken up with one session if, for instance, a project needs specific equipment.

PE

PE often takes place in the afternoon, either in the hall or outdoors. Insist on the children changing in silence and when they are ready sit them down on the carpet and explain the standards you expect in a PE lesson. Emphasise the reasons for keeping quiet in PE (safety and following instructions) and ask them to go out to the hall or onto the playground and stand in a space facing you. Take them through a warm-up, which will include stretching exercises and some aerobics. Then you will either be doing prescribed games 'this term it's tennis') or gymnastic activities. For health and safety considerations, unless you know the children well, don't let them use apparatus, apart from mats, benches and portable things like beanbags, hoops and skipping ropes. It is good (either indoors or outdoors) to get a carousel of activities going so that no child is doing the same thing for too long. Another form of activity, which is successful is educational gymnastics. This involves all the children in a graduated series of movements based, for instance on jumping, bridges or using space. You would need a copy of *Educational Gymnastics Step by Step*, which gives very explicit directions (Long, 1982).

At the end of the session do a warm-down so that the children have a chance to relax. One appropriate activity is to have them lying on their backs in a space on the floor, legs slightly apart, arms relaxed by their sides and eyes closed. Ask them to tense and then relax each part of their body in turn – head and face, shoulders, arms and hands, chests, stomachs and buttocks, legs and feet – breathing in and tensing for a count of four, holding for another count of four and then relaxing and breathing out counting four. Then tell them to get up slowly when they are ready and line up to go back to the classroom.

Out of school visits

You may find that your class has an out of school visit scheduled. This can involve anything from a quick inspection of the local church, a visit to the swimming pool or a whole day out. Whichever it is, you need a list of the class and the accompanying adults. Ideally, on whole days out you will have a ratio of one adult to six children, so divide them into groups, supply each adult with a list of the whole class and insist that each child stays with 'his' adult at all times. If there are enough adults, it is a good plan for you to take a "sheep dog" role: don't have a group of your own, but move among the groups, making sure that everyone is okay.

Activities and clipboards may be supplied for the children, but usually it is quite sufficient for them to enjoy the day without any constraints. Ask your adults to count their groups frequently and check up on the whole class as appropriate, but certainly as the children get on the bus and at dinnertime. And don't forget to take a bucket and wipes – children can get travel sick even on the shortest journeys and, if you're are not prepared for this, it can make for a miserable day.

END OF THE DAY

When it's time to end the afternoon's activities make sure that the children tidy the classroom before they sit down for a story. It's a good idea to get them to put all the things they need to take home (coats, bags, lunchboxes, reading folders and any letters home) ready on their tables, so that when it's time to go everything is in once place. I prefer not to read whatever the teacher is reading to the children at the moment. Partly because if it's a book I don't know, it's hard to read from the point of view of being able to understand the plot. But the main reason is that I have a good supply of stories. Some of them are in books, but if you can tell a story without a book, you're onto a winner. You can engage with the children more completely and, somehow, if you're telling a story they can suspend their disbelief. So, do try this. A favourite to tell younger children is the story of The Boy who cried Wolf! You can be quite noisy when you're crying 'Help! Help!' and you can even play the recorder a bit to show what the boy was doing while he was bored and looking after the sheep. When you've finished showing off, you can discuss the meaning of the story and how it relates to not telling tales all the time.

Another fun activity at the end of the afternoon is singing. This song is like "Heads, shoulder, knees and toes" in that each time you repeat the verse you leave out one more set of words and just do the actions.

Aunt Rebecca (clap, clap, clap, clap)
Climbed a tree (climbing mime)
Had a stick (clenched fists one on top of the other)
To boost her (bend your knees)
There she sat (fold your arms)
A-throwing stones (throwing action)
At my bob-tailed rooster (hands on hips and wriggle).

If you don't know the tune, it's just as much fun if you say it.

Another good activity is chanting "The Cookie Jar":

'Who stole the cookie from the cookie jar?'
'(Name one child) stole the cookie from the cookie jar.'
(Child who was named) 'Who? Me?'
(All) 'Yes, you!'
(Child) 'It couldn't have been!'
(All) 'Then who stole the cookie from the cookie jar?'
(Child names another child and the whole thing repeats from the start as many times as necessary. Great fun and the children always love it.)

To avoid a rush, it is a good idea to dismiss the children gradually. Older children can go table by table, but younger ones can go individually by birth months, colours of hair, eyes or clothes. It is essential that you make sure all younger children are collected.

If their parents or carers are late, bring the children back to the classroom and stay with them until someone comes for them.

Before you go, make sure that you have done all your marking and have left the classroom tidy. Marking is particularly important, because class teachers really appreciate it and are likely to ask for you by name when they need a supply teacher on another occasion. Leave a note for the class teacher about your day, remembering to note any concerns. And finally, don't forget to go to the office, otherwise you won't be paid.

Handy Hints

- Find out how your school's day runs.
- Check the school's behaviour policy.
- Listen to what you are told about the children, but trust your own judgement.
- Build up a good stock of your own resources.
- Look at your classroom to see how it is run.
- Write the date, your name and day's timetable on the board.
- Prepare a short board-based activity for the children;
- Greet the children when they come into the classroom and again by name when you call the register.
- Ensure that everyone is listening and looking at you before you start teaching.
- Remind the children about your expectations of acceptable behaviour and ensure you are consistent.
- Don't let the children change places, unless there is a valid educational reason for it.
- Use the children's names wherever possible.
- Let the children self-mark where appropriate.

- Make sure children are sitting quietly before you dismiss them.
- Try to have a short break for physical activity, even if it isn't officially timetabled.
- Use the staffroom as if you were a guest (which you are!).
- Use dinnertime to prepare your afternoon lessons and catch up on marking.
- Insist on a quiet PE lesson: do a warm-up, main activity and warm-down.
- For out of school activities make sure you have a full class list and separate adult-led groups.
- At the end of the day make sure the children have collected all the stuff they need to take home before they sit down for the story.
- Read your own book, tell a story or sing songs.
- Leave the classroom tidy and make sure you've done all your marking.

CHAPTER 4

RESOURCES AND OTHER PEOPLE'S LESSONS

If you are lucky, before you take on a class you will get a complete run-down on each lesson, itemising the different parts of the session and giving lists of groups of children for differentiation along with work for these groups.

The reality is that you will most probably be given a copy of the week's planning with highlights on it. You will have to scan the walls for lists of groups (which are different for literacy and numeracy) and work out which are the more and less able groups. (The best idea I came across was in one class where the more sides the group's shape symbol had, the more able the pupils were. The worst was where the able children were labelled gold and silver and the least able were in the black group. (Oh dear!)

On a good day, all the photocopies will be there for you; on a bad day you will be given pages numbers of a book which is somewhere on the desk...if there is a desk. There are some classrooms which have no discernible workstation, and the teacher is forced to hide all the accoutrements of the trade in seemingly random drawers and cupboards. Make sure you have everything you need before you start the lesson. If you have detailed instructions, follow them as closely as you can because the children will be used to a particular pattern of working and you will be less likely to have cries of *"Our* teacher never does that!"* (from *Please Mrs. Butler* (Alhberg, 2003). Failing any precise instructions, or when the school has given you a free hand ('We prefer our supply teachers to "teach to their own strengths"'), just follow the usual pattern of introduction, main part of the lesson and then a plenary.

If you are teaching to your own strengths (i.e., nothing has been prepared), try to give the children something which will be useful to them. (Cartoon of teacher with dumb-bells: teaching to own strengths) For example:

- A lesson on food miles (you will need a globe or world map), which challenge KS2 children to make a menu containing the most food miles and one using the least food miles.
- Road safety.
- Writing a letter, which means setting it out correctly and knowing your address (it's helpful if you get a copy of these from the office) including the postcode.
- Anything on the four rules of number, at an appropriate level.

- Measuring activities.
- Colour mixing and primary colours (KS1).
- Perspective (KS2).
- Writing instructions.
- Solids, liquids and gases (at different levels).
- If you have been told what the children are working on, it is possible that you have something appropriate, e.g. a Roman soldier to be labelled or a sheet about the 5 Ks (for unit on Sikhism).
- Haikus (based on a Japanese poetry form – each poem is three lines long: the first line is five syllables, second line, seven syllables and third line five syllables, traditionally on a theme of nature) enable all children to be successful poets and provide a really effective one-off lesson. See Patricia Donegan's book *Haiku* for more information.
- Quick and effective art activities, such as the starburst picture: take an A4 sheet of white paper, put two large dots in the middle and ten small dots randomly on the rest of the paper. Join each small dot to both large dots with two separate lines, using a ruler. Brightly colour in the resulting picture and cut out and mount on black sugar paper.

MODERN MATHS

When doing the four rules of number you must be aware of the relatively recent changes to the ways in which operations are carried out.

Addition

Children use the empty number line. This helps them to break numbers into parts before adding them up, for example by adding tens and then units onto the original number, e.g. $8 + 7$

$$+2 \quad\quad +5$$

$$8 \quad 10 \quad\quad 15$$

Children add the tens and then the ones to form partial sums, and then add these partial sums. The sums can be written horizontally or vertically, e.g. $47 + 76$

$$47+76=40+70+7+6=110+13=123$$

or

$$47 = 40 + 7$$
$$+76 = 70 + 6$$
$$\overline{110 + 13 = 123}$$

Subtraction

Using the empty number line, children can break numbers into parts before subtracting them, for example working back first to a multiple of ten, e.g. $74 - 27$

$$-3 \quad\quad -20 \quad -4$$

$$47 \quad 50 \quad\quad 70 \quad 74$$
$$\overline{3+20+4=27}$$

For larger numbers, the expanded layout helps children to understand the thinking behind the standard subtraction method.

Numbers are broken down into hundreds, tens and ones, ensuring that for each part of the calculation, the number on top is larger than that below. Each lower number is then subtracted from the one on top, e.g. 563-271

$$500 + 60 + 3$$
$$-200 + 70 + 1$$

This leads to

$$400 + 160 + 3$$
$$-200 + 70 + 1$$
$$200 + 90 + 2 \quad = 292$$

Multiplication

Children use the grid method. Numbers to be multiplied are split into ones, tens (and hundreds for three-digit calculations) and placed in a grid. The elements are then multiplied together and added up to reveal the answer, e.g. 56 x 27

x	20	7	
50	1000	350	1350
6	120	42	162
			1512

Division

This method is known as "chunking". Pupils subtract multiples of the divisor (usually multiples of ten) to find the answer. In time, they will learn to reduce the number of interim steps, e.g. 196/6

Leading to:

6) 196	6) 196
-60 (6x10)	-180 (6x30)
136	16
-60 (6x10)	-12 (6x2)
76	4
-60 (6x10)	
16	
-12 (6x2)	
4 (remainder)	
10+10+10+2=32, r4	30+2=32, r4

WHERE TO FIND RESOURCES

Your best source of materials is www.primaryresources.co.uk. All the work here has been contributed by teachers and co-ordination is done by Gareth Pitchford, who founded the site in 1998. Most areas have recommendations as to suitable ages for individual pieces of work (obviously it is up to you to find what is appropriate), but generally the site is very easy to use and you can spend a lot of time just browsing.

You can also find resources in the educational press such as *Early Years Educator* and *5 to 7 Educator*. These two provide a variety of stand-alone posters and worksheets, which are an absolute boon. *The Times Educational Supplement (TES)* supplies excellent ideas every week and has recently opened an excellent resource bank, free once you have logged on. You are encouraged to contribute to this site as well as downloading their resources – www.tes.co.uk/resources.

The other prime source of material is to be found in schools themselves. If you have found a piece of work particularly effective, take a copy of it or make a note of where it can be found. Because of the structure of the literacy and numeracy strategies, you will find that classes are studying the same subjects at the same time so, for example if you go into Year 2 classes in different schools during the same week, they are very likely to be studying identical topics.

You will also have your own favourite resources, so use them when you can. If something has worked particularly well in the past, your enthusiasm will shine through.

IF YOU DON'T FEEL ABLE TO TEACH A LESSON

Because this book is about the real world, there are occasions when you don't feel able to teach a lesson. There could be several reasons for this: one would be that the teacher has left you a really random instruction ("Let this Y5 class experiment with sand and water all afternoon"!). You feel that to comply with this would lead to mayhem at the least and you don't have immediate access to appropriate resources to make the activities meaningful.

"Follow the music lesson as set out in the book". Fine, except that the CD is missing. It's not even in the CD player.

"The children have been practising their sequences on the wall bars and ropes." Don't even go there. You don't know the children and their capabilities, and, after all, your first duty is to their health and safety.

So basically, if you lack knowledge, equipment or sufficient input, don't teach the set lesson. If there are any parallel class teachers, you could discuss the matter with them and ask their advice, or you could talk about it with the class TA, if appropriate. In any case, you now have to provide a replacement lesson. Try to keep to the same curriculum area, if necessary revisiting and expanding on a topic the children have already covered. Most teachers will be really pleased if you fill in with either a music or RE lesson, because those are areas in which they often feel they lack expertise, so it's useful to have some examples of these with you, just in case.

I always have a storyboard writing frame with me. This can be adapted to almost any age group, but you could always improvise. Get the children to fold an A3 sheet of paper (A4 will do, but obviously doesn't give so much space) long ways. Then they should fold that into three, giving six landscape-shaped rectangles. Ask them to use these rectangles to make a storyboard showing a picture and captions on each one. You can use this to fit all kinds of topics, or just ask the children to retell a well-known story.

Knowledge gap

You will sometimes find that you are expected to teach a lesson on something about which you know very little or nothing. Don't try to bluff your way through it; ask the children what they already know and say that it's a subject you haven't studied, but that you're looking forward to learning about, for example, the Aztecs. It's important that children should understand that learning is a lifelong process, not just something you do at school. I find they're usually rather surprised if I say, "I don't know –

how can we find out?". They seem to think that teachers know everything – wrong! Perhaps that's just the impression adults like to give.

Handy Hints

- Make sure you have everything you need before you start your lesson.
- If you are teaching a one-off lesson, try to ensure that you are teaching the children something useful.
- Be aware of recent changes in maths operations.
- Try to build up a good bank of your own resources, which can be found online, in educational magazines and in schools.
- If for some reason you are unable to teach a set lesson, replace it with something similar.
- Contrary to popular expectation, teachers don't know everything! Don't try to bluff your way through something with which you are unfamiliar, but ask the children how they think you can find out about it.

CHAPTER 5

CLASSROOM AND BEHAVIOUR MANAGEMENT

You need to remember that effective teaching leads to effective learning. Every teacher has a unique style and technique, but the following observations may be helpful.

You will always be involved with content: putting across a curriculum of knowledge and understanding, skills, attitudes, values and beliefs. You are responsible for the children you are teaching; the manager of their learning for the time you are with them, so it is up to you to make sure they will absorb as much as possible while you are with them.

THE CLASSROOM

One of the most important aspects is the classroom itself: how it is set out and how the available space is used. Different teachers have different priorities. Some may set great store by having a large carpet area, thereby sacrificing space between tables, while others prefer to be able to get between the tables more easily, thereby having ready access to the children while they are working. As a supply teacher, there is little you can do about how a classroom is set out, because making changes will cause a disproportionate amount of fuss. What you can do is make sure that children sit in their usual places (they will always ask you if they can move). The chances are that their teacher will have sorted out the seating very carefully, so there is no point in changing it and you might as well take advantage of what has been set in place.

CLASSROOM MANAGEMENT

Classroom management is the combination of all the arrangements and processes, which create and sustain an environment in which successful learning can take place. It encompasses the entire range of what teachers do. Teachers' behaviour and attitudes are of particular importance and they need to muster organisational and interpersonal skills to ensure that the pupils are fully engaged in learning. Kounin (1970) has identified four concepts of classroom management skills:

1. Awareness of the many things that are going on in the classroom at the same time; an ability to be aware of potential trouble spots and nip them in the bud.
2. "Overlapping" – being able to do more than one thing at a time.
3. Pacing – managing each part of the lesson well to ensure the momentum of pupils' work is maintained and that the best possible use if made of available teaching time.
4. Self-preservation. This is about self-confidence and how teachers project themselves in the classroom to show that they are in control.

Looking at these concepts can help to pinpoint any aspects, which you feel you may need to work on. With regard to (3), I find it is effective if you draw the whole class together to focus on something. It could be a good piece of work, 'I particularly like the way Dan has illustrated this', or to clarify a point that has caused confusion.

The Elton Report on discipline in schools (1989) identified the need for a positive approach, specifically:

- Encouraging good behaviour rather than simply punishing bad behaviour.
- Policies need to make a clear distinction between appropriate and inappropriate behaviour and should be clear on which behaviour is totally unacceptable.
- Teachers must be committed to, and work within, this positive approach.

The ABC model of managing behaviour

This approach suggests that by focusing solely on bad behaviour, you are unlikely to alter or reduce its frequency. Negative attention tends to reinforce difficult or unacceptable behaviour. So A, B and C refer to:

- A – antecedents
- B – behaviour
- C – consequences.

Antecedents

Antecedents concern:

- The school in relation to its culture and ethos.
- How adult behaviour is presented and expressed.
- The atmosphere of the classroom and how it relates to presenting a supportive and safe environment.
- The pupil's background, including specific physical, mental or neurological concerns.
- Differentiating the curriculum to provide continuity and progression.
- Styles of communication and body language used in the classroom.

■ Understanding of rights, rules, routines and responsibilities (the 4 Rs).

The 4 Rs

The 4 Rs help to provide a framework for success by building confidence, reducing conflict and tension and being supportive and corrective. They should be seen as fair and reasonable. Children understand the 4Rs in terms of:

• understanding the <u>rights</u> of others to learn
• seeing the need for <u>rules</u>
• accepting and conforming to class <u>routines</u>
• exercising appropriate <u>responsibility</u> for their behaviour.

Behaviour

■ How is challenging behaviour expressed?
■ Where does it fit in relation to personal, verbal, non-verbal and work-skills levels?
■ What is the goal of that behaviour? Is it attention-seeking? A demonstration of power? Or, escape-motivated?

Consequences

Consequences to inappropriate behaviour may be either major or minor, but they do exist, both for teachers and pupils.

■ As a teacher, how will you influence the consequences?
■ Will there be a successful outcome to your actions?

STRATEGIES FOR POSITIVE BEHAVIOUR MANAGEMENT

1. If you give children some control over the situation you are likely to encounter a refusal to do something.

2. Give children time to react and be clear about your expectations.

3. Acknowledge what pupils are saying, but insist on your expectations being met.

4. Avoid being negative. Rather than saying, 'You may not go out' say, 'You may go out as soon as you have finished that sum'.

5. With some attention-seeking behaviour it is better to ignore it and focus on another pupil who is doing, "the right thing".

6. Try and remind children about what they should be doing, rather than emphasising what they are doing wrong.

7. Remind the children about sanctions and consequences.

8. Defer discussions about bad behaviour. Say that you will see a pupil later. This deprives him of an audience, but lets everyone know that the matter is being taken seriously. You are more likely to have a favourable outcome in a one-to-one situation.

Handy Hints

- Remember: effective teaching leads to effective learning.
- You will be putting across a curriculum of knowledge and understanding, skills, attitudes, values and beliefs.
- Use the space in the classroom to the best advantage.
- Make sure the children sit in their usual places.
- Classroom management has the aim of enabling successful learning to take place.
- The four concepts of classroom management skills are awareness, multi-tasking, pacing and self-preservation.
- Always maintain a positive approach and avoid negativity.

- Be aware of ABC – antecedents, behaviour and consequences.
- Make sure everyone understands the 4Rs – rights, rules, routines and responsibility.
- Try to give children some control over outcomes.
- Give them time to react to instructions and be clear about your expectations;
- Ignore attention-seeking behaviour when possible and focus instead on a child who is "doing the right thing".
- Remind children about what they should be doing rather than what they should not be doing.
- Defer discussions about bad behaviour: don't give pupils the satisfaction of having an audience.

CHAPTER 6

WORKING WITH OTHER ADULTS

These days it is very unusual to be in a classroom without any other adult present. Most classes have at least a TA, and it is quite probable that some individual pupils will have one-to-one support. Basically, you will come across three kinds of TA: the first says, "We always do…", the second says "Would you like me to…?" and the third says, "I'm needed in another class", and disappears. The third is somewhat unfortunate, because a TA can be really useful to a supply teacher. He knows the ropes and can guide you as to just how the day goes, deal directly with children who don't take to change and generally "oils the wheels". The TA is there to be a support and will often take groups of children to do the work you have set. It is imperative that a TA stops when you ask the rest of the class to do so and encourages the group to listen to any whole-class input. I have had to suggest this to a TA who was hell-bent on carrying on what she was doing with her group and would talk through whatever I was trying to do. So, don't take it for granted that the TA will work in a way that is helpful to you. Try to discuss with the TA beforehand what you intend teaching.

You need to find out who will be supporting your SEN pupils, the kind of support they will be giving and their timetable. Ideally, you should liaise with the special educational needs coordinator (SENCO) and find out all you can about the children in your care. Unfortunately, this isn't always possible.

Research and inspections have shown that well-managed and well-trained learning support assistants (LSA) can make a significant difference to the progress of a class. Your TA will already have been allocated a particular role in the classroom, so you just have to be aware of what this is.

If you have a "Would you like me to...?" TA, then he is worth his weight in gold. The role of support staff is to help you make sure that each child plays a full part in every lesson. Ideally, you should brief them fully before each lesson, but in practice this isn't often possible. During your introduction to a lesson, ask support staff to work closely with children who need help by:

- prompting shy pupils
- explaining any phrases which aren't understood
- observing individual responses to inform the support they will give later in the session.

Very often a class will be split into four groups and you will oversee two of them and the TA will work with the other two. Ask the TA to:

- Ensure that the children understand the task correctly.
- Remind the children of the main teaching points.
- Question the children appropriately and encourage their participation.
- Look for and note any common difficulties the children have so that these can be addressed during the plenary.
- Provide the children with any resources they may need.

However, TAs are not the only adults who may be working in your classroom. Sometimes you will have parent volunteers. These can be brilliant or disastrous, so it's best if you give them a fairly simple task to start with, unless they have a clearly designated role, like listening to readers. In that case, let them get on with what they usually do. Sometimes parent volunteers will attempt to engage you in conversation and may make indiscreet observations. Just explain that you can't stop and talk now, much as you would like to. And remember that they may be just as indiscreet about you.

Be prepared to make use of the knowledge of any adults who regularly work with the class because they know the children and the classroom routines. Remember though, it is your responsibility to direct and manage the class.

You will probably meet specialist support teachers who will come into the classroom to work with individual children, either in an SEN or EAL capacity. These teachers will either help the children with work the class is doing, or they may be using a separate programme.

If an adult is new to the class, introduce him to everyone and make sure he understands about basic health and safety issues and behaviour management within the classroom. You can suggest that supporting adults:

- Encourage children to work problems out for themselves.
- Encourage children to work together.
- See mistakes as a necessary part of the learning process.
- Encourage children to ask and answer questions.
- Intervene if a group of children is getting stuck.
- Listen to children's ideas and encourage them to extend them.
- Make sure all members of a group participate.
- Try and ensure evenness within the group: boost withdrawn children and try to control the over-enthusiasm of dominant ones.
- Praise success and effort.
- Compare pupils' work with their previous efforts and emphasise the progress they are making.
- Ask you if they have any queries.

As class teacher, you will have to monitor the work of supporting adults. Keep eye on them and be prepared to intervene if you feel they need encouragement to work in a particular way.

There are some "adults" you might prefer not to have in the classroom: work experience students from the local high school. You might strike lucky and get one brimming with enthusiasm or, on the other hand, you might get someone like Gary. I caught a glimpse of the head walking through the school with this student during dinner time and when he brought him into my room I realised that he had not been able to offload him onto any other teacher. Gary had been a pupil at the school a few years earlier and obviously felt that this would be an easy option for work experience. He sat down with a group of Y3 boys and proceeded to wind them up and swear.

It could have been a long afternoon, but fortunately I managed to send him off to assist another teacher. In general, work experience students should be given very precise tasks within the classroom, preferably with a small group of well-motivated children.

Very often you will get students on teaching practice. They will take part of the timetable by agreement with the class teacher. At other times they will assist in the class or they will have PPA time. When they are preparing to take the whole class, ask them what kind of input they would like you to make. Legally you have to be present while they are teaching, but some prefer to do it all themselves, in which case you have to respect that. It is easier to team teach with students and, it can be quite a confidence boost because it makes you realise just how much you do know!

They will ask you for verbal feedback, in which case you need to be realistic but kind. As with children, praise anything you feel they have managed particularly well and do comment on the displays they have mounted. One problem teaching students often have, particularly younger ones, is the feeling that they need to befriend the children. This can make for issues with discipline, so I remind them that the children already have plenty of friends, but they do need a good teacher and adult role model. On occasion, students will confide in you that they are not getting the support they need from the class teacher. They really should address such concerns to their tutor or their in-school mentor, if they have one.

Apart from the adults who work regularly in your classroom, there are others who will visit from time to time. Some schools have individual governors assigned to each class, and they are quite likely to come into class. They will probably be quite familiar with the routines, so do ask them to take an active role, if they would like to.

While parents often come into school on a regular basis, you should not invite them in on an informal basis. Any parental involvement should take place as part of a school policy.

You may receive visits from peripatetic teachers (music, for example) or workers from different support agencies, advisors, educational psychologists, medical officers, different therapists or inspectors. As a supply teacher, all you have to do is make them welcome and ensure they have access to everything they need. Apart from the peripatetic subject teachers (e.g. music), who will usually come in to take the whole class, these visitors will generally be concerned with one particular child.

Handy Hints

- Remember that no matter who the other adults in your classroom are, it is your responsibility to direct and manage the class.
- Well-managed LSAs can make a significant difference to the progress of a class.
- Try to brief support staff before a lesson, if possible.
- Treat any adults in your classroom as part of a team whose aim is to assist the children to learn.
- Try to allocate parent volunteers tasks in line with their abilities and talents.
- Introduce unfamiliar adults to the class.
- Monitor other adults and be prepared to intervene if they seem to need some encouragement.
- Work experience students need very specific tasks.
- Students on teaching practice need support and encouragement. Most of them are hard-working and conscientious.
- Make all visiting adults welcome to your classroom and, if possible, involve them in the children's education.

CHAPTER 7

LOOKING AFTER YOURSELF

This is particularly important for a supply teacher, because no-one else will look after you. In a sense you have an easier time than an ordinary class teacher, because you don't have the on-going responsibility of a class or of belonging to a school, with the different pressures permanency entails. On the other hand, you have to cope with the uncertainty of employment and a permanent sense of not knowing what you are going to be doing from day to day. Also, you don't "belong" anywhere and don't have the support of colleagues

As teachers, we are trained to plan everything meticulously, so this "not-knowing" scenario can be very unsettling. There are mornings when the phone rings and I have to take an instant decision as to whether I should accept work or not. A fairly good incentive is to ask myself 'Would you like £100?'. Usually, the answer is "Yes, please!".

Congratulations! Having taken the decision to be a supply teacher, you have already taken a big step towards being able to get your work-life (or perhaps that should be life-work?) balance right. You will no longer have to work at weekends or in the evenings and you can have days off whenever you want to, or whenever your bank balance says you may. You can decide how much input you want to make; no-one will be persuading you to take after-school clubs, join focus groups or pursue further professional qualifications in your free time.

The Work-Life Balance Trust (W-LBT) was so successful in promoting the need for a work-life dialogue that it was able to disband in 2005, but it carried out some research, which showed

that failure to achieve the correct balance of effort and rest is
linked to a feeling of lack of control over your workload, plus lack
of energy to fulfil personal goals and commitments. If the balance
is wrong, the result may include fatigue, poor performance and
a poor quality of life. The W-LBT wrote a guide for women, but
I have altered it to include men, whose needs are just as essential
as women's.

Work-life balance guide

1. Be realistic. You *can* have it all, but probably not all at once.
2. Stop feeling guilty about your family. The guilt won't make
   any difference, except to your own psychological health.
3. If you have a family, make sure that each parent spends
   time with the children independently and each can then
   have a bit more "me-time".

4. Aim to be a bit healthier than you are at the moment.

5. Never buy a handbag (or a man bag) that isn't at least A4 size.

6. Plan your life on paper. Keep a diary and plan your weekend and evenings as carefully as you do your weekdays. Plan your day on an index card, with not more than 3 things to do and 3 telephone calls to make. If you add something, cross something else out. Make lists and cross off items as you do them. Delegate whatever you can. Even very small children can sort socks. Give your children responsibilities commensurate with their age and ability.

7. Learn to say "no". Don't take on too much and don't do things you don't want to. That sounds so obvious, but many people take on commitments because they think they should.

8. Keep saying "no". If something needs doing, then someone will do it, but not you.

9. If you feel constantly tired, take a day off away from home and on your own to rethink your goals. Take a note of your decisions.

10. You can't get a quart out of a pint pot, i.e. you can't do more than you can do. So don't beat yourself up. To achieve your work-life balance you need to develop a fast and adaptable sense of priorities.

These tips come from the Work-Life Balance Trust's Getting Personal, a 12-step, Girl's Guide to Personal Work-Life Balance. (http://www.w-lb.org.uk)

KEEPING HEALTHY

Eating and drinking

You will know that to stay healthy you need plenty of fresh fruit and vegetables as part of a balanced diet. You also need to drink large amounts of water (the tap variety is quite OK), which will also help to maintain your throat in good order and ensure that you don't get laryngitis. Try not to drink too much coffee and tea as caffeine can over-stimulate you. Many schools provide excellent salad options in their kitchens, so go for those if you can. If you have a school dinner, it also ensures that you do take a break. Try to keep below the recommended number of alcohol units (14 units a week for a woman, 21 for a man).

Exercise

Try to take regular exercise. Use your flexible timetable to make the most of using the local gym at off-peak times. You can usually get quite a good deal if you only go during normal working hours. You should aim to do aerobic exercise two or three times a week. This will help to keep your heart healthy and will enable you to keep your weight down. Aerobic exercise doesn't necessarily mean you have to don Lycra and a sweatband. It can be a simple as a brisk, 30-minute walk. Swimming is an excellent form of exercise as you can use all your muscles without the weight-bearing factor, which can cause strain on joints. A simple way of getting more exercise is just to think about whether you need to take the car out or not. Could you walk or cycle instead?

Rest

Most people need seven or eight hours' sleep every day, but you will know what suits you best. Almost two-thirds of people have difficulty sleeping. If you are one of them, here are some ideas which might help:

■ Go to bed and get up at about the same time every day.

■ Keep a pen and paper by the bed so that you can make lists of things you need to do and therefore stop worrying about them.

■ Make sure you get plenty of fresh air.

■ Take regular, moderate exercise, but not too close to bedtime.

■ Your bedroom should be well-ventilated, dark, quiet and not too warm.

■ Avoid excessive alcohol consumption as it is likely to interrupt your sleep.

■ Avoid coffee and tea in the evening as they are stimulants. They can stop you falling asleep and prevent deep sleep.

■ Don't eat too much late at night.

■ Have a drink of herbal tea or a hot, milky drink to help you relax.

■ Sprinkle lavender oil on your pillow.

■ Eat bananas and avocados: they are good sources of vitamin B, which helps sleep problems caused by adrenal stress.

■ Make love: it's very soporific and, in any case, more fun than lying awake or counting sheep.

■ Have a warm, not hot, bath.

■ Play mind games: counting sheep is a favourite, but you could imagine a room covered wall-to-wall and floor to ceiling with black velvet; describe your home town in the greatest possible detail; repeat 'Sleep, sleep, sleep' very slowly until you drop off.

- You can take sleeping pills, but they don't cause natural or restful sleep and can become addictive: only take them in the short term (and prescribed by your GP) to break an abnormal sleep pattern.

- If you can't get to sleep, don't just lie there: get up and do something for a while until you do feel sleepy and then go back to bed.

Relaxation

Relaxation is not just sleeping, but taking positive steps to relax during your waking hours. Practise your relaxation techniques. Try yoga, Pilates, the Alexander Technique and meditation. See what works best for you.

An occasional self-indulgent day is good. If you go to a health farm or spa centre for the day, take a friend and then you won't feel so guilty. You can try all sorts of treatments and, if there's one which particularly suits you, then you can make that part of your routine. An hour's massage isn't very expensive and it really chills you out and makes you feel good. Often colleges that train students in massage and natural therapies offer discounted treatments by students (these are supervised) so that they build up experience and the required practical hours to qualify.

Your life-work balance is important. After all, this is the real thing, not a rehearsal. Make sure that you take time to enjoy yourself. The exercise you take may or not contribute to your enjoyment, but do go to the cinema, concert or theatre regularly, keep in touch with your friends, listen to music, read books, go to evening classes, work with a charity or indulge in some retail therapy.

I can recommend a book, *Work-Life Balance: a Practical Guide for Teachers* by Margaret Adams (2006c). The author works in schools and gives much sensible advice to help with prioritising, delegation and managing your life. It contains an audit to help you assess the changes you need to make.

Smoking

Don't do it! If you are a smoker, try to give up. Schools are non-smoking areas, so getting your fix can be a frustrating and squalid experience. There are numerous sites on the internet to help you to stop smoking, but it seems that the most successful ones are based on replacement – replacement of nicotine with a substitute – and displacement activities. One of them suggests washing up, which is practical but not very exciting.

Support

If for any reason you find you can't cope, there is a charity you can contact for advice. It's called the Teacher Support Network and you can ring them on 08000 562 561 or visit their website – www.teachersupport.info.

MAKING THE MOST OF YOUR LIFE

As a supply teacher you have more opportunity than most people to do something exciting and different with your life. OK, you have the constraint of having to earn a living. You may have a family to consider, but you can plan to do at least some of the things you never had time for. Travelling, writing, painting, music, learning or charity work can be all fitted in if you take the trouble to organise yourself. A friend of mine is currently doing an MA while fitting in two or three days' supply each week – hard work, but well worth doing. It's up to you to make the time work for you. To quote Channel 4, "Time is the new money", so make sure you have a healthy bank balance.

Handy Hints

- Get your work-life balance right.
- Maintain a healthy diet.
- Drink plenty of water.
- Restrict your intake of caffeine and alcohol.
- Exercise regularly and use the gym at off-peak times.
- Go swimming.
- Don't always take the car – try walking or cycling.

- Make sure you get enough sleep.
- Slot in some relaxation.
- Have a massage.
- Give up smoking.
- Remember, time is the new money, so make the most of it.

BIBLIOGRAPHY

References

Adams M (2006c) *Work-Life Balance: A Practical Guide for Teachers.* David Fulton, London

Ahlberg A (2003) *Please Mrs. Butler.* Puffin Books, London

Department for Education and Skills (1999a) *National Numeracy Strategy.* DfES Publications Centre, Annesley, Nottingham

DfES, QCA (2000b) *National Curriculum Handbook for primary teachers in England..* QCA Publications, Sudbury, Suffolk

DfES (2000c) *Mathematical Challenges for able pupils in Key Stages One and Two.* DfES Publications Centre, Annesley, Nottingham

DfES (2001a) *Course for Supply Teachers, Returners to Teaching and Teachers from Overseas.* DfES Publications Centre, Annesley, Nottingham

DfES (2001b) *Teachers' Standards Framework.* DfES Publications Centre, Annesley, Nottingham

DfES (2001c) *Transforming Secondary Education.* DfES Publications Centre, Annesley, Nottingham

DfES, (2002a) *Self-study Materials for Supply Teachers: Pack (Getting Started, Core Subjects in Primary Schools, Core Subjects in Secondary Schools, Classroom and Behaviour Management and Filling the Gaps).* DfES Publications Centre, Annesley, Nottingham

DfES (2002b) *Special Educational Needs (SEN) Code of Practice.* DfES Publications Centre, Annesley, Nottingham

DfES (2006a) *School Teachers' Pay and Conditions Document 2006.* DfES Publications Centre, Annesley, Nottingham

DfES (2006b) *The Blue Book — Capital Funding for Voluntary Aided (VA) schools in England 2006–2007 Version*, DfES Publications Centre, Annesley, Nottingham

Donegan P (2004) *Haiku: Learn to Express Yourself by Writing Poetry in the Japanese Tradition*. Tuttle Publishing, North Clarendon, Vermont

The Elton Report (1989) *Discipline in Schools. Report of the Committee of Enquiry chaired by Lord Elton*. HMSO, London

Kounin J.S. (1970) *Discipline and Group Management in Classrooms*. Holt, Reinhardt and Winston, New York, NY

Local Government Employees (LGE) (2000a) *Conditions of Service for Schoolteachers in England and Wales (The Burgundy Book)*. LGE, London

Long B (1982) *Educational Gymnastics Step by Step*. Hodder Arnold H&S, London

Further reading and websites

Adams M (2006) *Work-Life Balance: A Practical Guide for Teachers*. David Fulton, London

Kounin J (1970) *Discussion and Group Management*. New York. Holt, Rinehart and Winston, New York

Long B (1982) *Educational Gymnastics Step by Step*. Hodder Arnold, Hodder and Stoughton, London

Books you may want to take into school

Ahlberg A (1983) *Please Mrs. Butler*. Puffin Books, London

Cookson P (ed.) (2000) *The Works*. Macmillan Children's Books, London

Crossley-Holland K (1998) *Short!*. Oxford University Press, Oxford

Donegan P (2003) *Haiku*. Tuttle Publishing, North Clarendon, Vermont

Patten B (ed.) (1998) *The Puffin Book of Brilliant Poetry*. Puffin Books, London

Rosen M (2005) *Fantastically Funny Stories*. Kingfisher Books Ltd., Boston, MA

Teaching unions

ATL (Association of Teachers and Lecturers)
www.askatl.org.uk 020 7930 6441

NASUWT (National Association of Schoolmasters and Union of Women Teachers)
www.nasuwt.org.uk 0121 453 6150

NUT (National Union of Teachers)
www.teachers.org.uk. 020 7388 6191

PAT (Professional Association of Teachers)
www.pat.org.uk 01332 372337

In each case I have given the number of the union's headquarters. They will be able to direct you to your local office.

Other websites

All accessed March 2007

Commission for Racial Equality – **www.cre.gov.uk**

For information on child protection –
**http://www.teachernet.gov.uk/wholeschool/
familyandcommunity/childprotection/child
protection.**

For information on physical restraint – **www.dfes.gov.
uk/publications/guidanceonthelaw/10_98/summary.
htm**

DfES Standards site – **www.dfes/standards/gov.uk**

Criminal Records Bureau – **www.disclosure.gov.uk**

The Disability Rights Commission – **www.drc-gb.org**

Equal Opportunities Commission – **www.eoc.org.uk**

Inclusion – **www.nc.uk.net**

EAL – **www.standards.dfes.gov.uk/ethnicminorities/
Conditions of teachers' employment** – **www.
teachernet.gov.uk/pay**

DfES supply teachers' website – **www.teachernet.gov.uk/
supplyteachers/**

DfES website – **www.teachernet.gov.uk**

Teacher Support – **www.teachersupport.info**

UK Street Map – **www.streetmap.co.uk**

Online resources

Primary Resources – **www.primaryresources.co.uk**

Resources for supply teachers – **www.supplybag.co.uk**

The Times Educational Supplement – **www.tes.co.uk/ resources**

Supply agencies

Most of these agencies have local offices, so I have just given their main numbers so you can find the office closest to you.

Capita – **enquiry.ers@capita.co.uk 0800 731 6871**

Career Teachers – **info@careerteachers.co.uk 0207 382 4270**

Eteach – **www.eteach.com**

Reed Education – **education@reed.co.uk 0208 680 4282**

Select Education – **education@selecteducation.com 0845 600 1234**

Stepteachers – **info@stepteachers.co.uk 0800 026 5198**

Teaching Personnel – **www.teachingpersonnel.com 01707 386 218**

TimePlan – **tes@timeplan.net 0800 358 8040**